IN A HOUSE OF SECRET ROOMS

TOM MORAN

ISBN: 978-93-6354-742-1

First Edition: 2025
Rs. 200/-

Cyberwit.net
HIG 45 Kaushambi Kunj, Kalindipuram
Allahabad - 211011 (U.P.) India
http://www.cyberwit.net
Tel: +(91) 9415091004
E-mail: info@cyberwit.net

Printed at QP.

For Christine,
who lets me see
life through her eyes

Like sealed rooms in a house, there are memories I try to avoid.
I did not want to revisit them. But I was not going to simply say
"Get over it. Forget it, that is all in the past".
The past is a formidable opponent. It is always there.
I learned that poems are hinges on doors to be opened.
I open these closed doors inside me, explore the rooms within;
to confront and accept, without flinching, what lies in yesterday.
I composed these poems to help me understand "why" things happened,
not as much as "how" they happened.
I conquer these buried griefs and anger.
I now enjoy all the rooms in my home.
Hopefully, you will see some reflection in your life.

Contents

My Soul is a Telegraph Vine

Straining to the top
it twists and spins
in a chain link fence.
Not a lily, a rose, or majestic flower
but a thin, resilient, ever persistent
orchestra schematic.
Not a palindrome,
a prime number in no particular order.
No questions asked in real life.
A flower of survival.
My birth is a reluctant mirror.
It sees what I should be
but I know where I'm at.
Time, a bootleg animal,
is laughing its ass off
with a big, evil grin.

Old Calendars

A New Year's tradition is to
throw out the old calendar
pin up a new one.
I review dates
from last year.
Dinner with friends
New Year's Eve at 6:00 P.M.
Cancer doctor's appointment
5/17 at 12:45.
Our anniversary 10/5.
Putting down two of our cats,
10/29 and 11/3.
Day I retired, 3/22.
I flip over pages of
a new calendar,
blank spaces
wait to be filled
like water
into an ice cube tray.
Next New Year's Day
I'll look back at mile posts
I leave behind.

Bridge Tender

I stand on the Riverwalk
in downtown Chicago.
Watch bridges tilt up
and boats go out.
How easy it is
to sit in a tower
push buttons to
raise and lower bridges.
But I allow only certain cargo
to pass on my river.
Raise and lower bridges
only when I have something to say.

My Father Waltzes in Heaven

My father once told me
"Don't be so gullible about people.
Remember it was people
that killed Christ and
you're sure no better than He was".
My father had a heart attack while driving home.
He was dead before he hit the steering wheel.
Police used a night stick
to break a window and
open his car door.
I called the police later to thank them.
The officer said, "We had to.
A crowd was forming.
They would have stolen his shoes".
Now that he has his shoes
my father can dance
whenever he needs to.

Now and Then

In the woods
I look for a place
I've been to before
but the view
is unfamiliar.
I can't find
that same spot.
Was it ever there
to begin with?
Has it changed?
Or am I trying
to remember something
that never was.
I see three deer
just feet from me.
I won't disturb them
because like the nearness
of an idea
a thought
or a love,
they will flee.
Stillness will vanish
nothingness remain.

Purple Heart

August 1970.
I'm eleven years old.
My mother takes me to see "Patton".
I ask why and she says
"Because I want you
to see how real men are,
not like your father."
After the first five minutes of the movie
I don't have ears left
on the side of my head.
I would later look up
what "fornicating" means.

Like home,
the movie has battle scenes
of hand to hand combat.
A scene where Patton
slaps a soldier
touches a nerve.
The soldier reveals
he "just couldn't take the shelling anymore".
He is sent back to the front.
I know that feeling in his stomach.
There are days I don't want to go home.
I don't want to go back to the front.

We walk back to the car.
My mother smiles.
I am sworn to secrecy.
I realize I have just enlisted and
am now a new platoon in a war.

How Far to Eden?

Out from this world
I will enter a garden
filled with my loved ones.
They will be transposed
into radiant flowers.
Iris and lilac,
dahlia, delphinium,
oriental lily and hyacinth,
rose of sharon and morning glory;
ringed by a barberry bush
which burns crimson in the fall.
Like a hummingbird
searching for sweet nectar
I will visit each flower
and make a haven.
Beauty will engulf me-
not as a sun shower
but forever.

My Brother's Phone

I still have John's black phone.
The one he would call me on and
talk of birthdays, Christmas, and Easter.
Black like a chalkboard
with "Do Not Erase" written on it.
He died lying on his kitchen floor for eight days.
The medical examiner threw a yellow blanket over him.
A field of sunflowers were in bloom
when I drove south
to clear out his apartment.
I can't toss his phone.
What if he calls me on it and
tells me of a warm afterlife.
My mother would melt butter on
the fresh Irish soda bread right from the oven.
I won't let go of the device we last talked on.
It is always fully charged.
We'll see each other again,
drink a broth of oblivion.

Lit Fest '24

A father holds
his daughter's hand
as she hops from
stone bench to stone bench.
When a gap is too far
he lifts her up
to leap across.
One day
she'll jump across
without his help,
but will still feel his pull.

Away

I write my poem
on a kite,
fly it
until I run
out of string.
Somewhere it lands and
someone will know
words come from above.

Play my "harp
by how I feel,
blow notes out
I'll never get back.
I push out
an inky black poison
of beatings I took
while keeping
my mouth shut.
Wounds heal
stitches hold.
I cross the street
catch up with my heart,
to feel again
trust again
create again

without toppling over.

Oasis

Stray cats come
to our home to feed.

"*Go to that house*"
they tell other cats.
"*God lives there.*
They put out food
like it's Thanksgiving.
They're strays too;
they know what it's like
scrimping by
on spotty portions".

Motion light trips on.
A fellow refugee to feed.
I open a fresh can.
For a flash
I know how God feels
granting tender mercies.

Shore Leave

Homes on my block
are silhouetted against
a cement wall
of the Chicago Skyway.
In winter, with furnaces on,
smoke curls out from chimneys
making houses look
like ships at sea.
After a movie
I walk home
through a viaduct
keeping an eye out
for large cars
with shark fins
and bumpers
that eat little children.
An older boy stands at one end,
won't let me pass.
He says "This is my viaduct and you can't enter".
He swings at me and misses.
I unload on him
with everything I have
because with bullies
you only get one shot.
He walks away
massaging his cheek
mumbling "I didn't think he'd hit me".
But I can't linger.
I have to get back to my ship
and join my crew.

Relay

A spider spins a web for survival.
If the web is destroyed
it rebuilds because
the spider needs to eat.
I spin a web to snare poems.
If none are caught
I spin a wider web
because I need to heal
to understand
to let go.

Will my poems end up
in a thrift store along with
old furniture, dishes,
forgotten jewelry?
Or are they tracks
leading nowhere.

Perhaps pages
will fly loose
scatter in the breeze.
Maybe someone
will put their foot
on one page
pick it up
read it and say,
"I feel that too".

Outside the Box

Our parish priest died
when I was seven and
laid out in the church
during school hours
so kids could say goodbye.
When it's my turn
I look down
see his open eyes,
pale blue marbles
staring outward.
How strange
a robust, strapping man
confined to a little box.

My brother passed,
cremated.
He is 6'8" but reduced
to a package sent home
through the mail.
At his service
he is put in an urn
then the ground.
After my mother's funeral
I clean out her condo.
Photos in a bin;
frozen images of when
we were a family.
Those containers are in a
storage unit-
a box
within a box
within another box.

On my leaving day
I'll be a bird
on a wire
waiting for a certain breeze.
My spirit rising on thermals.

Tiny Diamond

Twinkle twinkle
little star
I wonder
how far
you are
from me.

You were close
when I dreamed
of what
could be
but you are
farther and farther away
as I am older
and my road has narrowed.

Someday my ashes
will be scattered
on this rock
circling the Sun.
In the dark,
a traveler
made of stardust,
I will yield to
when God
hammered out
the universe
like a mystical blacksmith.
Sparks flew
and stars
were born.

On the Shelf

Excuse my safari hat.
It has a flap on the back
which shields me from
an indifferent sun.
It covers a scar
when a melanoma was removed.
The surgeon razored
living tissue off my scalp
to graft over a slice.
I don't have a flap
large enough to cover
other holes in me.
There's a poem here somewhere.
But the clerk at the bookstore
says poetry doesn't sell.
I say, "It's not supposed to sell;
it oozes out from festering wounds.
Here is my book of scars".

I'm told poetry
is evidence
presented in court.
The reader renders a verdict.
I present my evidence.
"Here is my book of scars.
If it doesn't sell
let it escape".
Because the clerk
at the bookstore
says poetry doesn’t sell.

Controlled Burn

Prairie grass
high fives me
as I walk
the path I've chosen.
I collect seeds
because like poems
seeds do not travel,
they must be carried.
I gather words
in the morning after
moisture dries off,
bring my thoughts
to sow in open fields.
I torch piles of underbrush
monopolizing sunlight,
weed out tears and grief
allowing new growth.

Grass sways
wind letting me know
it was here.
My poems waver
on the page
letting you know
I was here.

Amen

When I was thirteen, I had my tonsils removed.
The night before surgery I tossed and turned but couldn't fall asleep.
About 1:00 A.M. I heard keys jingling at the door. A small man in a housekeeping uniform came in with a mop, bucket, and a dry dust mop.
He began sweeping next to my bed. "How are you doing?' he asked.
I told him I was nervous and having a hard time falling asleep.
He said "Don't worry. Everything will be okay". After sweeping, he mopped the washroom and as he left he said "Get some sleep. You'll be alright".
Comforted, I drifted off.

In the morning a nurse came in to take my vitals. She asked how I slept.
I told her I was restless at first but after I talked to a housekeeper, I fell right off.
She asked what time this was and I said about 1:00 A.M.
The nurse said "There are no housekeepers on duty after 11:00 P.M.
Why would he clean around your bed only? And at 1:00 A.M.?
I don't know who that was."

Wooden gate opens
A wondrous garden revealed
Feel what is unseen

Two Rivers

I live in the land
between two rivers;
one dreamed
one real.

What is dreamt?
What will I use for paper
when I can no longer write.
What will I use for air
when I can no longer breathe.
How can I feel
when I will not be able to touch.

What is real?
Rising every morning
in a house that's paid for.
Awakening to create,
to find words that describe
a fragment of hurt
I see in a mirror.
My wife Christine
kneading top soil
in her garden.
We as children at play
in a culture of sun.

When these rivers merge
our spirits,
carried by a steady current,
will live in the silt
of a welcoming delta.
Absorbed by clouds
to return as rain
our souls will be
two raindrops
on a windowpane
sliding into one.

Seeds

I stand outside of church
hoping God won't see me.

I toss seed on the ground,
watch sparrows as they
peck around.

My spirit scatters out,
water escaping a failed dam.

Reading other poets
I look for a spark
that prompts a prairie fire.

Inside, pews, slivers of salvation,
let me sleep safely.

As birds feed
I search for that one seed,
one ember.

No words, music, or incantations;
just sweet acceptance
of my transient soul.

Pruning

I'm sorry I chopped
your clematis by mistake.
I was intensely cutting
creeping charlie and
mistook your flower for a weed.
You pointed out the clematis
before I started
but I think of some people
some problems
lose my head and
just cut away.

You've taught me the difference
between weeds and flowers
since we've been together.
You always could see
a flower in a patch of weeds.
I work to keep creeping charlie
out of garden
out of our lives
prune it from my poems.
A never-ending battle
to keep hijackers at bay.

One Good Turn

I was a night custodian
at an elementary school.
The man I replaced, John,
came in for a couple of nights
to show me the ropes.
He had to resign
because his prostate cancer
had carried to his organs.
It spread as hot embers
on a windy night
jumping from house to house to house.

I visited John
when he was brought home to hospice.
He threw out anger like lawn darts.
"Why me? What did I do to deserve this?
Who'll take care of my wife and kids!"
John knew he would be gone soon.
We talked in undeniable terms.
He thanked me for not snowing him by saying
"You'll beat this. You'll get better".
John said it's an insult to tell someone who is dying
"You'll pull through".
I shook his hand.
The line of bottled meds next to him
looked like a firing squad.

Three weeks later
I attended John's wake.
Consoled his wife and children,
walked past photos of John
as a young man in the Navy in "Nam.
I stood next to his casket
delivered a load of prayers and thanks.
My bill of lading left unsigned.

Unafraid

Multiple words
begin with "un"-
undiscovered, unadorned, unappreciated,
unknown, unanswered,
unseeing, unspoken, unrealized.
I marry words
with my life's station.
Try what's untested, unyielding, unvoiced,
unnamed, undaunted, unused.
Race towards an understanding
of undeniable faith.

Preserves

In July
take a Mason Jar
and bottle some sun.
Place that jar
on a shelf
in your basement.
On an arctic January morning
go to the basement
open the jar-

"Ah, summer!"

Acknowledgements

Illinois State Poetry Society
Poems appear on ISPS web site
and ISPS Anthology *Distilled Lives*

University of Iowa Summer Writing Festival
Thanks to Staff and other poets

Poetry Foundation
Chicago, Il.

Michael Escoubas
Editor, *Quill and Parchment*

Jacob Erin-Cilberto
John A. Logan College
Southern Illinois

Dr. Bakul Banerjee
Editor *Naperville Writers Group*
Naperville, Il.

Westmont Library
Westmont, Il.

Barbara's Bookstore
Lombard, Il.

Prairie Lights Bookstore
Iowa City, IA.

Haunted Bookstore
Iowa City, IA.

Brewed Awakenings Coffee Shop
Westmont, IL.
Thanks to Sylvia, Karen, Craig, Bruce and Frank
Numerous poems were birthed there.

Dam on !st Ave, over the Iowa River
Iowa City, IA.
True inspiration

www.ingramcontent.com/pod-product-compliance
Ingram Content Group UK Ltd.
Pitfield, Milton Keynes, MK11 3LW, UK
UKHW040038200726
13845UKWH00054B/466

9 789363 547421